SPOT'S BIRTHDAY PARTY

First performed at the Oxford Playhouse on 6th April 2000, and on tour, including a London season at the Lyric, Hammersmith. The play was produced by Hedda Beeby and Tish Francis for Oxford Playhouse Productions, with the following cast:

Steve	Matthew Harvey
Sam/Musical Director	Alexander L'Estrange
	(*Lyric, Hammersmith only*) Adam Rowe
Tom	Daniel Robinson
Spot	Dale Superville
Marco	Daniel Tomlinson
Sally	Joanna Van Kampen

Mouse Puppeteers	Aaron Bixley, Charley Pugsley

Directed by **David Wood**
Designed by **Will Hargreaves**
Director of Movement **Jack Murphy**
Musical Supervisor **Paul Knight**
Lighting by **Tim Boyd**
Magic Consultant **Geoffrey Durham**
Sound Designer **Graham Naylor**
Assistant Director **Fiona Ingram**

CHARACTERS

Spot, a puppy—lovable, bouncy, always learning
Steve, a monkey—funny, acrobatic, boisterous, sometimes silly
Tom, a crocodile—shy yet enthusiastic, a little slow to join in things
Sam, Spot's father, who also plays keyboards
Marco, a rabbit—extrovert entertainer
Sally, Spot's mother
Helen, a hippo—spirited but sensible, sometimes a bit bossy, loves ballet dancing

A puppet **Mouse**, operated by stage management

MUSICAL NUMBERS

ACT I

WHERE'S SPOT?	Sally, Sam, Tom, Helen, Steve
WELCOME TO MY PARTY	Spot, Tom, Helen, Steve, Sally, Sam, Marco
SPOT'S BIG BAND	Spot, Tom, Helen, Steve, Sally, Sam, Mouse
PASS THE PARCEL	Marco, Sally, Spot, Tom, Helen, Steve

ACT II

LIKE A STATUE	Marco, Sally, Sam, Spot, Tom, Helen, Steve, Mouse
HAPPY BIRTHDAY, SPOT	Sally, Sam, Tom, Helen, Steve, Marco, Spot
THANK YOU SONG	Sally, Sam, Spot, Steve, Tom, Helen, Marco

CURTAIN CALL

HAPPY BIRTHDAY, SPOT	All except Spot
HOPE YOU LIKED MY PARTY	All

Music

The vocal/incidental music, arranged by Paul Knight, is available from Samuel French Ltd

Cover illustration

Permission to use this illustration, or any other Eric Hill illustration, should be obtained from Salspot Limited, 80 The Strand, London, WC2R ORL.

Eric Hill's SPOT books are published by Penguin.

Photograph

The photograph of the original Oxford Playhouse production is by Robert Day and remains the photographer's copyright.

The following billing must be used in all advertising in connection with this play

SPOT'S BIRTHDAY PARTY
adapted for the stage by David Wood
from the books by Eric Hill

and both names shall appear in the same size type and neither name shall be mentioned without the other.

INTRODUCTION

The challenge was to create an exciting introduction to theatre for children of pre-school, kindergarten and reception class age—the age group for which the *Spot* books and television programmes are aimed—as well as their parents, teachers and slightly older siblings. We employed a cast of six actors (four male, two female), all of whom were versatile; singing, character movement, occasional acrobatic and circus skills, plus the ability to connect with a children's audience were vital. Our musical director/keyboard player was on stage, playing Spot's father. A puppet Mouse was operated by stage management.

For many years Spot has been a favourite character of very small children. Although he is a puppy, and his friends are also young animals, his adventures reflect the early experiences and learning progress of small children. The stories appear to be extremely simple, but relate perfectly to the children, who recognize themselves and the everyday activities they grow up with. This age-group would find it difficult to follow a sophisticated through-line plot. But it was necessary to impose a shape on the entertainment to make it a satisfying experience, complete with a beginning, middle and end.

A birthday party offered a recognizable structure, even to the youngest children. Guests arriving, the giving of presents, the playing of games, the presence of an entertainer, the tea complete with cake and candies to blow out, and the going-home thank-yous offer familiarity and the chance, especially in the games, of audience participation. The show could be an event, a celebration. The children in the audience could be guests at the party rather than simply spectators of a performance. For many children this would be a first-time theatre experience and making it an invitation to a birthday party would instil excitement and anticipation.

The posters, leaflets and tickets were all designed as invitations rather than direct publicity. Children were encouraged to bring a home-made birthday card for Spot. Some children even put on their party outfits.

One of the most successful aspects of the *Spot* books is the use of flaps revealing surprises. Our designer ingeniously found ways to interpret this theatrically. One-dimensional objects—a table, a dressing-up chest—suddenly became three-dimensional as the characters pulled them out of the wall. The one-dimensional clock had a door which opened to reveal a hiding place. Other key objects designed to look like the book illustrations included a pink baby grand piano, Spot's dog basket, a window with a window box, a Welsh dresser and a bookshelf. These were all integrated into a room setting, reflecting the colours, clear lines and simplicity of Eric Hill's distinctive style. Four "blocks" were used, to stand or sit on. They were like children's building blocks, with letters, geometric figures and numbers on their sides. During the show they were repositioned as appropriate. At the end, the blocks spelt SPOT.

To make the characters exactly resemble the book illustrations would have been virtually impossible, unless the actors' faces were hidden and their movements restricted. Our designer's solution was to create headdresses which faithfully reproduced the familiar animal heads and which sat on top of the actors' heads, allowing their human faces to be seen. Using the familiar colours, costumes were designed which reflected current children's and adult fashions, and incorporated animal tails echoing the book illustrations. The audience completely accepted the actors as the characters.

This was in no small measure due to the excellent character movement developed with the cast by our Director of Movement. Each actor found an appropriate style of movement based on the animal they were playing, yet taking into account that the human, childlike qualities of the character were equally important. For instance, Helen's movement combined hippo weightiness with human ballet-dancing steps, and Marco developed enthusiastic rabbit hops.

Our magical advisor helped Marco, the rabbit entertainer, perform some magic tricks, and he also learned how to create a balloon animal resembling Spot. In this acting edition we are prevented from revealing the workings of the tricks by the rules of the Magic Circle. Future directors of the play should consult a local magician for help in this area. Incidentally, our Marco's extrovert performance was enhanced by an Italian accent.

An important aspect of the Spot concept is early learning. Colours, counting, stories, growing things, telling the time and the playing of percussion instruments were all incorporated into the play, not overtly, but within the party framework. For instance, we found several places when the characters could play percussion instruments not only to accompany songs, but also as incidental sound effects in the *Cinderella* storytelling. Incidentally, the *Cinderella* sequence was also "educational" in that Spot and his friends acted out the story, putting on clothes from the dressing-up box and using objects already seen to become things in the story: for example, Spot's ball became the pumpkin, and the triangle used in Spot's Big Band was used to create the chimes of the clock.

Every child received a going-home present—we provided a baseball-style hat made of thin card, which advertised the show! Other productions might consider giving each child a piece of birthday cake or a balloon.

David Wood

The cast of the Oxford Playhouse production

Photo: Robert Day

ACKNOWLEDGEMENTS

Eric Hill and Salspot Ltd generously allowed me to create a new character for this play—Marco, the rabbit entertainer. Thanks to them, also, for their encouragement and confidence in the development of this adaptation.

I would also like to thank Hedda Beeby and Tish Francis for commissioning this play and for producing it so splendidly. Their support and enthusiasm for the project was echoed throughout every department of the Oxford Playhouse, making *Spot's Birthday Party* a real pleasure to bring to the stage.

David Wood

OTHER PLAYS AND MUSICALS BY DAVID WOOD

Aladdin
The BFG (based on the book by Roald Dahl)
Babe, the Sheep-Pig (based on the book by Dick King-Smith)
Babes in the Magic Wood
Cinderella
Dick Whittington and Wondercat
Dinosaurs and all that Rubbish (based on the book by Michael Foreman)
Flibberty and the Penguin
The Gingerbread Man
Hijack Over Hygenia
The Ideal Gnome Expedition
Jack and the Giant
Jack the Lad (co-written with Dave and Tom Arthur)
Larry the Lamb in Toytown (co-written with Sheila Ruskin, adapted from the stories of S. G. Hulme-Beaman)
Meg and Mog Show (from the books by Helen Nicoll and Jan Pienkowski)
More Adventures of Noddy (based on the stories by Enid Blyton)
Mother Goose's Golden Christmas
Noddy (based on the stories by Enid Blyton)
Nutcracker Sweet
Old Father Time
The Old Man of Lochnagar (based on the book by HRH The Prince of Wales)
Old Mother Hubbard
The Owl and the Pussycat went to See... (co-written with Sheila Ruskin)
The Papertown Paperchase
The Pied Piper (co-written with Dave and Toni Arthur)
The Plotters of Cabbage Patch Corner
Robin Hood (co-written with Dave and Toni Arthur)
Rupert and the Green Dragon (based on the Rupert stories and characters by Mary Tourtel and Alfred Bestall)
Save the Human (based on the story by Tony Husband and David Wood)
The See-Saw Tree
The Selfish Shellfish
There Was An Old Woman...
Tickle (one act)
Tom's Midnight Garden (based on the book by Philippa Pearce)
The Twits (based on the book by Roald Dahl)
The Witches (based on the book by Roald Dahl)

Theatre for Children—Guide to Writing, Adapting, Directing and Acting (written with Janet Grant, published by Faber and Faber)

ACT I

As the audience enter the auditorium, the stage decor is visible. There are four doors, each a different colour—green, blue, brown and yellow (with a brown spot): these colours echo the characters' colours. The doors could be portable screens, but in the original production they were linked together to enable them to be folded to become a magic cabinet

Children's birthday cards to Spot are visible either side of the stage or on the proscenium arch

Music 1 (Pre-recorded tunes from the show)

The front of house staff, wearing party hats, greet the audience. Perhaps they collect birthday cards for Spot brought by the children. In the original production, the children were invited to place their cards in a dog basket in the foyer

A few minutes before the start of the show, the company manager brings the cards to the stage and carefully displays them in Spot's basket, to the side of the stage

The pre-recorded music and the House Lights fade

Sam and Sally enter. In the original production, Sam played a piano accordion in this section

Music 2

Sam and Sally greet the audience, speaking in rhyme

Sam I'm Sam, Spot's Dad...
Sally I'm Sally, Spot's Mum...
Sam & Sally We're so glad that you could come.
Sam It's party time!
Sally It's time to play!
Sam & Sally To celebrate Spot's special day!
Sam Are you ready?

Audience Yes!
Sally Are you steady?
Audience Yes!
Sam Then ... wait a minute, Sally, where is he?
Sally Where's who?
Sam Where's Spot? He should be here. It's his party.

They look around

Sally I can't see him. (*To the audience*) Can you see Spot?
Audience No.
Sam Let's look for him!
Sally Come on, everyone, help us find him!

Music 3

Song: Where's Spot?

Sally & Sam Where's Spot?
Where's he got to?
Where's Spot?
Where can he be?
Where's Spot?
Where's he got to?
Where's Spot?
Let's go see.

Sally goes to the doors

Is he behind the green door?
Let's knock three times and see

Sally knocks on the green door, encouraging the audience to join in

Knock, knock, knock!
Who's there? (*She opens the door*)

Tom enters, shyly excited

Tom   It's me!
(*Speaking*) I'm Tom.
Sally Hallo, Tom.
Tom Hallo. (*He looks around*) Where's Spot? I've brought him a present.
(*He hands the present to Sally*)

Act I

Sally We're looking for him. Help us, Tom!
Tom Right you are.

Sally leaves Tom's present on the floor

All   Where's Spot?
          Where's he hiding?
          Where's Spot?
          Where can he be?
          Where's Spot?
          Where's he hiding?
          Where's Spot?
          Let's go see.

They go to the doors

Tom   Is he behind the blue door?
Sally   Let's knock three times and see…
          (*Speaking, encouraging the audience to join in*) Come on, everyone!

Tom knocks on the blue door

All   Knock, knock, knock!
Sally & Tom Who's there?

They open the door. Helen enters, confidently

Helen   It's me!
          (*Speaking*) I'm Helen.
Sally & Tom Hallo, Helen.
Helen Hallo. Where's Spot? I've brought him a present. (*She hands her present to Sally*)
Sally & Tom We're looking for him. Help us, Helen!
Helen Of course.

Sally leaves Helen's present with Tom's

All   Where's Spot?
          What's he up to?
          Where's Spot?
          Where can he be?
          Where's Spot?
          What's he up to?

Where's Spot?
Let's go see.

Helen leads the way to the doors

Helen   Is he behind the brown door?
All   Let's knock three times and see…

Helen knocks on the brown door

All & Audience   Knock, knock, knock!
Who's there?

They open the door

Steve enters, acrobatically

Steve   It's me!
(*Speaking*) I'm Steve!
All Hallo, Steve!
Steve Hallo. Where's Spot? I've brought him a present. (*He holds up his hand and realizes he isn't holding anything*) Oh. Sorry.

Steve somersaults back out of the door, then returns with the present

Here it is.
Sally (*taking the present and adding it to the others*) Thanks, Steve.
Steve Where's Spot?
All We're looking for him. Help us, Steve!
Steve Okey dokey!
All   Where's Spot?
What's he doing?
Where's Spot?
Where can he be?
Where's Spot?
What's he doing?
Where's Spot?
Let's go see.

Steve leads the way to the doors

Steve   Is he behind the yellow door?
All   Let's knock three times and see…

Steve knocks on the yellow door

All & Audience Knock, knock, knock!
Who's there?

The music builds up the expectation that this time Spot will appear. The door opens

Marco enters, carrying his bag of equipment

Marco   It's me!
All (*surprised*) Who are you?
Marco Is this the party? I'm the entertainer!

All cheer

Sally Come in, come in!
Marco Thank you, madam. Marco's the name...

Music 4

Marco produces a bunch of flowers and hands it to Sally. Gasps

...magic's my game. Da daaaaa!

Cheers and applause

Sally Thank you, Marco.
Marco Now, where's the birthday puppy? It's party time!
All We can't find him.
Marco But no birthday puppy, no birthday party.
Sally Exactly.
Marco We must find him.
All But how?
Marco By...

Music 5

...magic!

All react excitedly

(*With dramatic gestures*) Lights!

The Lighting changes magically

Music!

Music 6

Magical music begins

Watch!

Marco directs the others to help him rearrange the four doors to make a four-sided cabinet

(*Placing the others* DS) Stand by! (*He takes out a magic wand. Remembering, he whispers*) What's the birthday puppy's name?
All (*whispering*) Spot.

Marco waves his wand and wiggles the fingers of his other hand

Marco   Abracadabbage
                 Carrot and pea
                 We want Spot
                 When we count to three. (*He encourages the others to count*)
All One, two, three!

Marco gingerly approaches the front door of the cabinet and peeps inside. He shuts it quickly

Marco Ah!
Steve It didn't work.
Marco Oh dear!

Everyone is disappointed

Wait! To make the magic stronger, please, let's— (*taking in the audience*) *all* say the magic spell. Everybody wiggle your fingers ... and say after me... Abracadabbage...
All Abracadabbage...
Marco Carrot and pea...
All Carrot and pea...
Marco We want Spot...
All We want Spot...
Marco When we count to three.

All When we count to three.

Marco leads the count

One, two, three!

A sudden flash

Then out of the cabinet comes Spot

The Lighting brightens

Marco We did it!

Cheers as Spot runs round greeting everybody, including the audience

NB: at this point in the original production, Steve and Tom pushed the magic cabinet to one side, enabling the puppeteer to secretly enter it from off stage

Spot Hallo, Tom! Hallo, Helen! Hallo, Steve! Hallo, Mum! (*If Sam is playing the keyboards*) Hallo, Dad!

The others wave and call out "Happy Birthday". Spot sees the audience

(*To the audience*) Hallo!
Audience Hallo!
Spot HALLO!
Audience HALLO!
Spot Thank you for coming to my party.

Sally indicates the birthday cards

Sally Look, Spot. Look what they've given you.

Spot goes to look

Spot Wow! Thanks for all these cards. They're brilliant!

All applaud the audience

(*Seeing Marco*) Hallo. Who are you?
Marco (*with a bow*) Your entertainer!

All cheer

Marco's the name...

Music 7

...magic's my game! (*He magically produces a plain-coloured scarf*) Da daaaaa! For you.
Spot Thank you! A scarf. (*He takes it and looks at it. Doing so he shows both sides to the audience*)
Marco Not just any old scarf. And these too. (*He shows Spot some paper spots in his hand*)
Spot (*taking them*) What are these?
Marco Spots. Please throw them.

Spot throws the spots in the air above the scarf. Suddenly, as the spots fall, the scarf is covered in spots

A spotty scarf for Spot! Da daaaaa!
Spot Thank you, Marco.

All applaud and cheer. Spot ties the scarf round his neck then goes to show it off to the others. As he moves, a squeaking sound is heard, accompanying each step he takes. NB: in the original production at this point Sam, with his accordion, exited to take his place at the keyboards

Mouse Eek! Eek! Eek! Eek!

Spot stops and reacts, then starts again

Eek! Eek! Eek! Eek!

All watch and listen

Eek! Eek! Eek! Eek!

Spot looks at his feet. The squeaks continue, no longer accompanying Spot's steps. All try to track down the noise

Eek! Eek! Eek! Eek!! Eek! Eek!
Spot (*softly*) What is it?

Suddenly, unseen by Spot and his friends, but in full view of the audience, Mouse (a glove puppet, not too small) pops up above the magic cabinet and waves cheekily

Mouse Eek! Eek!

Spot and his friends freeze. Hopefully the audience, having seen Mouse, call out to tell Spot

Eek! Eek!
Audience Mouse! Mouse!

Spot and his friends react to the audience

Spot What? A mouse? Where?

The audience point to Mouse. Spot and friends start to turn round. But Mouse disappears behind the screen before they see him. They turn back to the audience, looking bemused

There's no mouse!

Mouse appears again

Mouse Eek! Eek!

A couple more times Spot and his friends, led by the audience, turn, but just miss Mouse. Eventually Spot and his friends see Mouse. Spot approaches

Spot Hallo, Mouse.
Mouse Eek! Eek!
Spot What are you doing?
Mouse Eek! Eek! Eek!
Spot Squeaking? Yes, we heard you!
Mouse Eek!
Spot Can't you speak?
Mouse Eek!
Spot No, only squeak?
Mouse Eek!
Spot Oh dear, I can only understand speaking, not squeaking.

Mouse squeaks a few bars of "Happy Birthday to You"

(*To the others and the audience*) What's he squeaking?

Hopefully the audience understand

Audience Happy birthday to you!

Spot Happy birthday to me?
Mouse Eek!
Spot Well, thank you, Mouse.

Mouse excitedly squeaks as he descends into the magic cabinet

Bye bye!

Mouse excitedly squeaks as he reappears, carrying a tiny birthday card

Hallo, again!
Mouse Eek! (*He hands Spot the card*)
Spot What's this?
Mouse Eek! Eek! Eek! Eek!
Spot A birthday card! Well, thank you, Mouse, that's very kind. I'll put it
right here. (*He attaches it somewhere visible—in the original production
on the Welsh dresser*)
Mouse (*pleased*) Eek!
Spot Welcome to my party!
Mouse Eek! Eek!

Marco comes forward

Marco Come on, everybody, let's party! (*He signals for music to start*)

Music 8

*Spot's friends take the magic cabinet and Mouse off stage. During the
following song, Mouse appears elsewhere and dances happily, while Spot
and his friends encourage the audience to join in, waving and dancing in their
seats and doing the appropriate "actions". Disco Lighting effects*

Song: Welcome to My Party
Spot   Welcome to my party, party, party
Come on in and join in all the fun
Welcome to my party, party, party
Welcome ev'ryone!

(*Speaking to the audience*) Let's dance! Come on, everyone. Stand up if
you want to. And dance along with us!

First
Let's all hold our hands up high

	Move to the music, reach for the sky!
All	Left, right, left right, left right
	Wheee!

Welcome to the party, party, party
Come on in and join in all the fun
Welcome to the party, party, party
Welcome ev'ryone!

Spot encourages Tom and Steve to lead the next "action"

Tom & Steve Next
Sway your tails like Steve and Tom
Swing to the music, bom diddy bom!
All Swing, sway, swing, sway, swing, sway
Wheee!

Welcome to the party, party, party
Come on in and join in all the fun
Welcome to the party, party, party
Welcome ev'ryone!

Spot encourages Helen to lead the next "action"

Helen (*slower tempo*) We're
Feeling hot so let's get cool
Swim in the water, splash in the pool!
All Splish, splash, splish, splash, splish, splash
Wheee!

Welcome to the party, party, party
Come on in and join in all the fun
Welcome to the party, party, party
Welcome ev'ryone!

Spot (*speaking*) Come on, everyone, let's do *all* the actions!
All Left, right, left right, left right
Wheee!
Swing, sway, swing, sway, swing, sway
Wheee!
Splish, splash, splish, splash, splish, splash
Wheee!
Welcome to the party, party, party

Come on in and join in all the fun
Welcome to the party, party, party
Welcome ev'ryone!

As the song ends, with a big cheer, music continues as Tom, Helen and Steve collect their presents and hand them to Spot

   Mouse exits

Tom Happy birthday, Spot!
Helen Happy birthday, Spot!
Steve Happy birthday, Spot!
Spot Thank you.

The parcels are piled one on top of the other, so Spot cannot see over the top. He walks precariously, nearly bumping into the others, who change his direction for him. Finally, he has to be rescued from nearly walking off stage

Sally Why don't you open your presents now, Spot?
Tom & Helen & Steve Yes! Open! Open! (*Etc.*)
Spot (*suddenly*) I know!
All What?
Spot Why don't I open my presents now?

All laugh and cheer. Spot takes a present

Tom That's from me. Guess what it is!
Spot Well, it's round. (*He presses it*) It's squeezy. (*He bounces it*) It's bouncy. (*He looks at the audience*) It's a...
Audience Ball!

Spot quickly takes off the wrapping paper

Tom Yes!
Spot What shall we play? (*He has an idea*) I know!

Music 9

The four friends play with the ball. An amusing interlude to music. In the original production they played "Pig In The Middle", in which Tom reluctantly was the "pig". Then Steve tried to balance on the ball, falling off a couple of times before Spot and Helen supported him, enabling him to travel on the ball by walking on it. Finally, Tom, who had felt a little left out, took the ball from under Steve's feet, making Steve, Spot and Helen fall over. Then he demonstrated his skill at holding the ball on his outstretched palm and twisting it right round his body without dropping it. Another idea would be for the friends to try to keep the ball off the ground while revolving round each other and crawling between each others' legs. The interlude should not last too long

Thanks for the ball, Tom. What's next? I think I'll open ... this one!
Helen That's from me! What do you think it is?
Spot Well ... it's square. (*He turns it over*) And it makes a noise. (*He shakes it*) It rattles! (*Looking at the audience*) It's a...

Hopefully the audience suggest ideas

A puzzle? A shaker?
Helen You'll never guess!
Tom and Steve Open it!
Spot Yes. (*He takes off the wrapping paper, revealing a large box of sunflower seeds*) It's... (*mystified*) lovely. What is it, Helen?
Helen A box of seeds. Sunflower seeds. You have to plant them in the earth. Then they grow into beautiful sunflowers.
Sally Perfect for the window-box, Spot. Why not plant them now?
Tom & Helen & Steve Yes!

Music 10

They hurry to fetch the window-box from us

Spot (*opening the box*) Thanks, Helen.

Spot's friends bring the window-box. Spot carefully plants the seeds

Now what?
Helen Put them in the window so they get lots of sunlight.
Spot & Steve & Tom Right!

They return the window-box to the window. Suddenly Mouse appears from behind the window-box

Mouse Eek! Eek!
Spot Hallo, Mouse.
Mouse Eek! Eek! Eek!
Spot What are we doing?

Mouse Eek!
Spot Planting seeds to grow sunflowers.
Mouse Eek! Eek! Eek!
Spot What's the matter?

Mouse disappears and returns with a small watering can

What's that?
Mouse Eek! Eek!
Helen It's a watering can.
Tom He's saying don't forget to water the seeds.
Steve They need water as well as sunshine.
Sally (*producing a larger watering can*) Here you are, Spot.
Spot Thanks, Mum. (*To Mouse*) Good idea, Mouse! (*He starts to carefully water the seeds*)
Helen   Water the seeds
                   To make them grow
                   See if they're growing
                   Are they?
All (*looking*) No!
Spot We could all say that. (*To the audience*) Come on, everyone.

Music 11

All & Audience Water the seeds
                   To make them grow
                   See if they're growing
                   Are they?
                   No!
Sally They won't grow that quickly!
Steve Hey, Spot. Why don't you open my present now?
Spot Yes, please, Steve.

All dash DS *to find the present*

Steve Guess what it is!
Spot Well, it's round at the top, and round at the bottom. (*He shakes it*) But it doesn't make a noise.
Steve Yes, it does! You have to bang it!

Spot bangs it

Spot I know what it is! (*He looks at the audience*) It's a...

Audience Drum!

Spot takes off the wrapping paper

Spot Yes! It's a drum! (*He happily bangs it*)

Sam, at the keyboard, takes up the rhythm

Music 12

Marco comes forward

Marco (*in rhythm*) Come on, friends, it's time to play
In Spot's big band! Spot, take it away!

Song: Spot's Big Band

As the song progresses, Marco hands percussion instruments and toy instruments to Spot's friends. They hold them behind their backs until the last moment to give an element of surprise. In the original production, Marco positioned himself by Sam's pink grand piano, where he had put his entertainer's "kit" upon arrival. Sally and Marco join in all the choruses, and, with the others, echo the actions made by each character playing an instrument

Spot   Some people like playing in the sea
Or playing in the sand
But as for me
I like to be
Playing in a band

(*Playing his drum*) Brum, brum, brum-brum-brum!
Brum, brum, brum-brum-brum!

(*Speaking*) Come on, everyone, drum along with me!
All & Audience   Brum, brum, brum-brum-brum!
Brum, brum, brum-brum-brum!

All   Spot's big band
The best band in the land!
Steve   May I play
In your band?
Spot   Yes you may

> Course you can
> What will you play
> In my band?

Steve   I'll play the trumpet

> Doo-doo doo-doo doo-doo doo doo!
> Doo-doo doo-doo doo-doo doo doo!

(*Speaking*) Come on! Everyone!

All (*led by Steve*) Doo-doo doo-doo doo-doo doo doo!
> Doo-doo doo-doo doo-doo doo doo!
> (*Led by Spot*) Brum, brum, brum-brum-brum!
> Brum, brum, brum-brum-brum!

> Spot's big band
> The best band in the land!

Helen   May I play
> In your band?

Spot   Yes you may
> Course you can
> What will you play
> In my band?

Helen   I'll play the triangle

> Ting ting ting-a-ling-a-ling
> Ting ting ting-a-ling-a-ling

(*Speaking*) Everybody!

All (*led by Helen*) Ting ting ting-a-ling-a-ling
> Ting ting ting-a-ling-a-ling
> (*Led by Steve*) Doo-doo doo-doo doo-doo doo doo!
> Doo-doo doo-doo doo-doo doo doo!
> (*Led by Spot*) Brum, brum, brum-brum-brum!
> Brum, brum, brum-brum-brum!
> Spot's big band
> The best band in the land!

Tom   May I play
> In your band?

Spot   Yes you may
> Course you can
> What will you play
> In my band?

Tom   I'll play the cymbals

*Tom's cymbals should be real ones, large enough to make a big sound.
Coming from the shy Tom, this has a humorous surprise effect on everybody*

        Clap, clap, clap, clap
   (*Speaking*) Everybody!
All (*led by Tom*) Clap, clap, clap, clap
        (*Led by Helen*) Ting ting ting-a-ling-a-ling
        Ting ting ting-a-ling-a-ling
        (*Led by Steve*) Doo-doo doo-doo doo-doo doo doo!
        Doo-doo doo-doo doo-doo doo doo!
        (*Led by Spot*) Brum, brum, brum-brum-brum!
        Brum, brum, brum-brum-brum!

        Spot's big band
        The best band in the land!

*Suddenly Mouse appears. In the original production he popped up above the
clock*

Mouse Eek! Eek! Eek!

The others register

Steve It's Mouse!
Tom He wants to join the band!
Helen Can he, Spot?
Spot Course he can! Your turn, Mouse! Squeak away!
Mouse   Eek! Eek! Eek! Eek! Eek! Eek!
        Eek! Eek! Eek! Eek! Eek! Eek!
Spot (*speaking*) Everybody!
All (*led by Mouse*) Eek! Eek! Eek! Eek! Eek! Eek!
        Eek! Eek! Eek! Eek! Eek! Eek!
        (*Led by Tom*) Clap, clap, clap, clap
        (*Led by Helen*) Ting ting ting-a-ling-a-ling
        Ting ting ting-a-ling-a-ling
        (*Led by Steve*) Doo-doo doo-doo doo-doo doo doo!
        Doo-doo doo-doo doo-doo doo doo!
        (*Led by Spot*) Brum, brum, brum-brum-brum!
        Brum, brum, brum-brum-brum!
        Spot's big band
        The best band in the land!
Spot Last time! (*To the audience*) Play whatever you want to play!

Final chorus, in which all make their noises together! A jam session! Perhaps

Spot and his friends march around and then stand on the blocks for a big finish

> Spot's big band
> The best band in the land!

Marco (*speaking*) Let's give a big hand
> For Spot's big band! Da daaaaaa!

All applaud each other and the audience

Mouse disappears

Music 13

> And now, my friends, if you kindly sit…

Spot, Steve, Tom and Helen sit on the blocks

> It's time for me to do my bit!

The following is optional…

Sally notices all the wrapping paper on the floor

Sally I'd better clear up. (*She goes to pick up the wrapping paper*)

Marco stops her

Marco Wait, madam! (*He picks up the carrier bag in which he brought his kit, inverts it and holds it up in one hand*)

Music 13a

With his other hand he makes magic passes towards the bag

> Abracadabbages! (*From the bag he magically produces a long-handled broom*) Da daaaa!

All cheer. Marco hands the broom to Sally

Sally Thank you, Marco! (*She uses the broom to sweep off the wrapping paper*)

Sally exits

In the original production, this sequence was made possible by a special magic trick provided by our magic advisor! If it is impracticable, Sally can simply pick up the wrapping paper and exit as Spot and his friends sit down

End of optional material

Marco performs. Perhaps he does some magic. Perhaps he juggles. This section should, however, be relatively passive for the audience—something interesting and attractive to watch rather than direct audience participation. In the original production, Marco handed out one balloon each to Spot and his friends

Marco   One balloon each, my friends, please blow!
              One at a time, off you go!

Music 14

Steve blows up his balloon. Marco watches. The balloon is shaped like a bird. Steve shows it off

Steve It's a bird! (*He lets it go*)

It flies off

    It flew away!
Marco Never mind! (*He goes to Helen*) Helen?

Helen blows up her balloon, then releases it. Her balloon is the kind that flies more slowly than normal, because it has a tube to restrict air escape. Perhaps it makes a noise too

Helen It's dancing!
Marco (*going to Tom*) Tom!

Tom blows, making a loud raspberry noise. His balloon has a large hole in it. He tries again. Another raspberry. He shakes his head. Marco shakes his head in sympathy and proceeds to Spot

    Spot?

Spot produces a blown-up long yellow modelling balloon and hands it to Marco. (He has either blown it up himself, or substituted the balloon Marco gave him for a blown-up one) Marco, in his children's entertainer role, takes the balloon and fashions it into a puppy shape. Finally he takes a sticky-backed brown spot and places it on the balloon puppy's side. He holds up this model of Spot

Da daaaaa!

Cheers and applause

Happy birthday, Spot!
Spot (*taking the balloon model*) Thank you, Marco. (*He shows it off*)

NB: In the balloon sequence it was originally intended to use all modelling balloons. These offer the possibilities of one starting to grow from the bottom or another curling as it is blown up. However the cast found it impossible to blow up these special balloons without risking a heart attack! So we found some novelty balloons in a party shop. These probably worked better anyway, because they were different shapes and more fun. Marco, of course, did use a modelling balloon to fashion a "Spot" model, but even he didn't need to blow it up, as explained above

Suddenly Mouse appears on the bookshelf

Mouse Eek! Eek! Eek! Eek!

All react

Spot It's Mouse. Where is she?

All look

Mouse Eek! Eek! Eek!

The audience direct Spot and his friends to Mouse

Spot There you are! (*To the audience*) Thank you! (*To Mouse*) Hallo, Mouse. Look what Marco gave me! (*He leaves the balloon model on the shelf*) What's up?
Mouse Eek! Eek! Eek!
Helen He says we ought to water the seeds again.
Spot Yes! (*He fetches the large watering can*)

All watch as he waters

Come on, everyone!

Music 15

All & Audience Water the seeds
                    To make them grow
                    See if they're growing
                    Are they?
                    No!

Sally enters, carrying a parcel

Sally I've told you, they won't grow that quickly! (*She gives Spot the parcel*)
           Spot, you've got one more present!
Spot Thanks, Mum. What is it?
Sally I don't know. It's from your grandparents.
Spot (*feeling it*) It's quite soft.
Sally That's because they've wrapped it in lots of layers of wrapping paper.
Spot Why?
Sally So you and your friends can play...
All (*realizing*) Pass the Parcel!

Music 16

Spot and his friends clear the blocks, if necessary, form a circle and start passing the parcel. Sally watches. Marco supervises

Song: Pass the Parcel
All   Pass the parcel
                   Pass the parcel
                   What's it going to be?
                   Pass the parcel
                   Pass the parcel
                   Pass the parcel

This phrase is repeated until Marco blows his whistle, or, as in the original production, his harmonica, with which he also accompanied the song

        Open it and see!

Tom is holding the parcel. Urged on by the others, he removes the top layer of paper. He is disappointed to find another layer

Spot (*encouragingly*) Your turn, Tom.

Tom starts the parcel's journey again, passing it this time around the outside of the circle

All   Pass the parcel
                   Pass the parcel
                   What's it going to be?
                   Pass the parcel
                   Pass the parcel
                   Pass the parcel (*Etc.*)

Marco whistles

                   Open it and see!

Helen is holding the parcel. She excitedly removes the next layer of paper. Another layer is revealed

Spot Your turn, Helen.

Helen decides to pass the parcel between her legs. The others pick this up

All   Pass the parcel
                   Pass the parcel
                   What's it going to be?
                   Pass the parcel
                   Pass the parcel
                   Pass the parcel (*Etc.*)

Marco whistles

                   Open it and see!

Steve is holding the parcel. He quickly removes the next layer of paper, revealing another

Spot Your turn, Steve.

Steve passes the parcel over his head, or in another inventive way

All   Pass the parcel
                   Pass the parcel
                   What's it going to be?
                   Pass the parcel

> Pass the parcel
> Pass the parcel (*Etc.*)

Marco whistles

> Open it and see!

Spot is holding the parcel. He removes the paper, revealing a large book—
"Spot's Storybook"

Spot   It's a book! For me!

Tom I like books!
Helen It's a book of *stories*!
Steve I like stories!
Helen So do I.
Spot What stories are in here?
Sally (*looking over Spot's shoulder*) It's got *Puss in Boots, Snow White,
    Hansel and Gretel, Cinderella...*
Helen Cinderella, that's my favourite story!
Steve Is that the one with the princess and the pea?
Helen No, but there's a prince and a pumpkin!
Tom What's a pumpkin?
Spot A big vegetable!
Helen Yes, and Cinderella has two horrible stepsisters...
Steve (*remembering*) And a Fairy Godmother!
Helen Yes!
Sally Listen, why don't we all tell the story of Cinderella? Spot, you could
    read it and we could play it out? Marco?
Marco Do our own play? Why not?
Spot (*going to the dressing-up chest*) We've got some dressing-up things.
    Come on, everybody, let's get ready!

Music 17

Music as everybody prepares, dressing up and finding props. We hear
occasional lines: "This could be the pumpkin" regarding the ball; "Can I be
Cinderella?" from Helen; "Where's Mouse? There's a mouse in the story";
"Here's a magic wand for the Fairy Godmother"; "Does the prince need a
crown?", etc.

Eventually everyone is ready. If possible, all should remain on stage and
enter the story when necessary. The sound effects are all created by Marco
and the others, using percussion instruments, in view. The sequence should

*resemble the way children act out stories at home or at playgroup, but with
an extra theatricality and sophistication, to excite and involve the audience's
imagination*

*The "costumes" should be very simple—identification factors rather than
fully realized costumes. As the Prince, Spot could wear a cardboard crown.
Cinderella could wear an apron and her ball gown could be a shawl or a
party dress. The stepsisters could wear skirts. The transformation of the
pumpkin/Mouse to coach should be simple yet magical*

Marco Lights!

Music 18

*A dramatic Lighting change, engineered by Marco, who acts as stage
manager from now on, and plays percussion instruments as sound effects*

Music!

In the original production, Helen played the flute for this introductory music

Spot comes forward with the storybook

Spot (*reading*) This is the tale of Cinderella,
Welcome, I'm your storyteller.
The curtain rises on scene one
When Cinders' life is not much fun.

Helen steps forward and mimes the following line

She does the dishes, cleans and cooks,

Helen tries to take the book from Spot. Spot walks away

She has no time for reading books.
The only friend who comes to call
Is Mouse, who lives behind the wall.

*He indicates and Mouse pops up. In the original production he appeared on
the dresser*

Helen   Hallo, Mouse!
Mouse   Eek! Eek! Eek! Eek!

Helen	Dear Mouse, if only you could speak.
	Would you like a piece of cheese?
Mouse	Eek! Eek! Eek!
Spot	That means, yes please!
	Suddenly they hear a roar…
Tom & Steve	Cinderella!

Tom and Steve "enter"

Spot	Through the door…
Helen	My stepsisters! They're very mean…
Marco	Burst upon the happy scene.

Music 19

Helen	Hallo, sisters.
Tom & Steve	That's enough!
	Watch your tongue or we'll get rough!
Tom	Brush my hair! Press my dress!
Steve	Cinders, dear, you'll never guess!

Marco hands Steve an invitation

	We're off to the Palace Ball tonight,
Tom	We'll be the prettiest girls in sight!
	Isn't it exciting news?
Steve	Paint my nails! Polish my shoes!
	We'll meet the Prince, we're so excited.
Tom (*taking the invitation and waving it in Helen's face*) What a shame you're not invited!
Spot	Cinders' friend thinks that's unfair.
Mouse	Eek!
Spot	That nasty pair deserve a scare.
Mouse	Eek! Eek! Eek!
Tom	Hey, look, what's that?
Steve	A mouse! A mouse! Aah! Fetch the cat!
Mouse	Eek! Eek! Eek!
Tom	A mouse! Oh no!
Steve	Come on, sister, quick, let's go!

Music 20

Tom and Steve hurry off

Helen   Thank you, Mouse, you've made me smile.
                    They won't be back for quite a while!

Music 21

Marco makes a "knock knock" sound

                    Who's this? Who's making such a din?
Sally (*"off"*) A poor old woman! Let me in!
                    Please give me shelter from the storm.

Helen mimes opening the door—Sally "enters", stooping under a cloak

Helen   Of course, come in, you'll soon feel warm.
Sally   Thank you.
Helen   Wait, a storm, you say?
                    There isn't any storm today!
Sally   And there's no poor old woman really,
                    Just someone who loves you dearly.
                    See my child, I am none other.
                    Than your Fairy Godmother!

Music 22

*A magical sound effect as Sally stands. Her cloak falls off as Marco hands
her a wand with a star*

Spot   Cinders gets a big surprise.
Helen   Gosh! I don't believe my eyes!
Sally   Your life so far's been truly tragic,
                    You deserve a bit of magic.
                    What's your greatest wish of all?
Helen   To dance tonight at the Palace Ball.
Sally   No problem, dear, you *will* go there!
Helen   But I've got nothing nice to wear!
Sally   That's easy! I just chant my spell——
                    Hey presto!

Music 23

*Magical sound and Lighting effect. Marco quickly helps Helen into her
ballgown and slippers. (NB in the original production two stars were fixed
to Helen's shoes, to save time)*

	Didn't I do well?
Helen	Godmother, gosh, what can I say?
Sally	Nothing, just be on your way.
Helen	How do I get there?
Sally	Don't you fuss!

You think I'd let you go by bus?
Fetch that pumpkin,

Helen fetches Spot's ball, placing it on the dressing-up chest

Mouse come too.

Helen collects Mouse and places him by the pumpkin. Music as Sally waves her wand

Abracadabra Wallaballoo!

Magical Lighting and sound effects. Marco magically makes a horse and coach appear, taking the place of Mouse and the pumpkin. This could be a hobby horse and a cut-out coach. (NB in the original production a cut-out rocking horse and a large version of a child's playcart rolled magically in through the door)

Spot   A coach appears, and that of course
              Is drawn by Mouse, turned into a horse!

Helen stands behind the horse, or in the cart

Helen   Godmother, thank you, thank you so!
Sally   Be back by midnight! Off you go!

Music 24

"Clip clop" sound effect as Helen is helped by Marco across the stage

Spot   Rumble, clatter, through the night
              Above the moon is shining bright

Lighting effect

              As Cinderella in her coach
              Sees the Palace gates approach.

Helen exits

Take your partners! Music play!

Music 25

The Palace Ball is under way.

Sally and Marco dance. Tom and Steve dance

The Prince is there but he's not dancing.

Spot looks up, but no-one is playing the Prince

(*Dropping the narrator's stance, whispering*) Mum, we haven't got a Prince!

Sally and Marco stop dancing

Sally (*taking the book from him*) *You* play the Prince, Spot.
Spot Me?

All whisper "yes"

All right then.

Marco places a cardboard crown on Spot's head

Music 26

Sally (*narrating*) The Prince is there but he's not dancing.
                  The two stepsisters start advancing.

Tom and Steve approach Spot

Tom	Princy, Princy, we're both free!
Steve	Dance with me!
Tom	No, me!
Steve	No, me!
Spot	Ladies, please, how could I choose? I think it's best if I refuse.
Tom	What a cheek!
Steve	He's very rude!
Tom	Let's go stuff ourselves with food!

They exit

Music 27

Helen enters

Sally   Cinders causes quite a stir.

Spot welcomes Helen

                 The Prince has only eyes for her.
                 There's nothing either needs to say
                 Entranced they dance the night away.

Spot and Helen dance. Music. The Lighting increases on the clock

                 Cinders loses track of time

Marco makes tick-tock noises as the clock hands turn through several hours towards midnight. They could be manipulated by one of Spot's friends

                 Until the clock begins to chime.

One of Spot's friends plays the triangle, chiming twelve times

                 Godmother's words ring in her head.
                 Be back by midnight, she had said.

The music stops

Helen   I'm sorry, sir. I cannot stay,
                 It's midnight! (*She backs away*)
Spot   Hey, don't run away!
Sally   But it's too late, she starts to run.

Helen starts to go. This could be done in slow motion

                 She knows the magic is undone.

Music 28

Helen throws off her "ball gown", or Marco helps her

                 Her rags return as she escapes.
                 The Prince is stunned, he stands and gapes.

Helen exits

Spot   Come back, I never asked your name!
                Come back!
Sally   But back she never came.
                He runs outside.

Spot exits

                        All he can find…

Spot returns, with one of Helen's slippers

Spot   One slipper she has left behind. (*He freezes, looking at the
                    slipper*)
Sally   The horse becomes the Mouse once more…

*Mouse, carried by one of Spot's friends, enters (or is seen against the
window)*

                He scuttles through the stable door.
Mouse   Eek! Eek! Eek!
Sally   He squeaks in fright
                And scampers homeward through the night.

Mouse exits

Music 29

Helen enters

Helen   Where's my coach?
Sally   Cries Cinders.
Helen   Where?

Marco rolls the pumpkin (ball) towards her

Sally   But only finds the pumpkin there.
Helen   Never mind, I had such fun,
                Forget the coach, I'll have to run!

Helen exits

Music 30

Sally   The Prince gives forth a proclamation.

Spot unfreezes

Spot   A search there'll be across the nation.
                   For I'd be truly thrilled to bits
                   To find the foot this slipper fits.
                   The girl who owns that foot will be
                   The girl I'll ask to marry me!

Cheers and applause. Spot walks purposefully on the spot

Sally   The Prince sets off upon his quest,
                   From North to South, from East to West.

Sally plays an "eager girl"

                   Each eager girl the slipper tries

Sally sits. She and Spot mime slipper-trying

                   But finds, "It's simply not my size".
                   The Prince's hope is fading fast
                   But Cinders' home he finds at last.

Music 31

Tom and Steve enter

Tom   Oooh! Sister, dear, the Prince is here!
Spot   Ladies, I had no idea.
                   That *you* lived here!
Steve   Oh yes, we do!
                   And we'd both love to marry you!
Sally   The poor old Prince begins to wonder
                   If he hasn't made a blunder.
Spot   Try the slipper, then, let's see…
Tom   I'll go first!
Steve   No, me!
Tom   No, me!
                   If it fits, I'll be your bride!

Music 32

Tom sits on a block and tries on the slipper

	It's not fair! My foot's too wide!
Steve	My turn! (*He tries the slipper on*)
	Ow! There's something wrong!
	My foot won't fit, it's far too long!
Spot	Sorry, ladies, not your day!
	Now I'd best be on my way. (*He turns to go*)
Sally	Suddenly Mouse dashes out.

Mouse appears, perhaps on the dresser

Tom	Shoo!
Steve	Shoo!
Sally	The sisters shout.
	But Mouse won't go! He has to stay!
	For he has urgent things to say.
Mouse	Eek! Eek! Eek! Eek! Eek! Eek!

Spot approaches Mouse

Sally	The Prince can't understand one squeak.
Mouse	Eek! Eek! Eek!
Spot	I beg your pardon!

Music 33

Helen enters

Sally	Then Cinders runs in from the garden.
Spot	Am I dreaming? I feel sure
	That I've seen you somewhere before.
Tom	Rubbish! Her?
Steve	No way! No chance!
	She was never at the dance!
Helen	My name is Cinderella, sir.
Tom	The kitchen maid, don't talk to her!
Sally	By now the Prince has wobbly knees.

Music 34

Spot	See this slipper? Try it, please.
Sally	Her heart goes pitter, patter, pitter,
	She tries the slipper, will it fit her?

Music 35

Helen tries the slipper on

              Yes, it fits! Like a dream!
              Mouse is thrilled. The sisters scream.
Tom & Steve Aaaaaah!!
Tom   Sister, dear, what are we in for?
Steve   At least we'll have a royal in-law!

Music 36

Spot goes on one knee

Sally   The Prince proposes, and guess what?

Helen nods

              Cinders accepts him on the spot!
              The wedding bells ring out next day.

Spot and Helen kiss

              The happy couple kiss and say…
All except Spot & Helen They'll love each other all their life,
              The Prince and Princess, man and wife.

Confetti is thrown. Cheers. Sally closes the storybook

    And that's the end of the story.
Tom (*worried*) Is it the end of the party as well?
Sally No, it's time for Spot's birthday tea!

Cheers

    Come on, everyone!

Music 37

Sally leads everybody off. Spot stays behind

Spot (*to the audience*) We won't be long! We'll be back soon for more games AND my birthday cake! See you soon!

Spot waves and follows the others off

END OF ACT I

INTERVAL

While Spot and his friends are supposedly having tea, it would be fair if the other party guests—the audience—could be given some "tea" too. The ideal thing would be to supply them with ice cream. This could involve sponsorship and may prove impractical! But if it is possible, Spot could announce that everybody, during the break, will receive a birthday ice cream

Music 38 (Recorded)

Music could play through the interval and the Pre-Act II activity

Optional Pre-Act II activity:

Before the start of Act II, with the House Lights still up, Spot and his friends return, playing with various toys—for example, a pedal car, a hobby horse, a unicycle, a space hopper, a pogo stick, a skateboard, a wheelbarrow, a hula hoop, roller blades. The sequence could start with Steve entering, cheekily finding Marco's juggling balls and trying to juggle. Marco could catch him and then start teaching him. All enjoy themselves, showing off, falling off, etc. This section would be worked out using particular skills of the performers

ACT II

The House Lights fade as Sam enters. He starts to play his keyboard

Music 39

Marco takes centre stage to introduce a game

Sally enters and joins in

Mouse pops up too, perhaps by the window-box

Song: Like a Statue

Marco   Come on, ev'rybody, on your feet
It's time to play a game that is kind of neat
You dance and prance and bounce until
I blow the whistle
And you all stand still!

(*Speaking*) Dance, dance and wait for the whistle! (*To the audience*) And
I want all of you to help me see who moves!

*The music continues. Spot and his friends dance. Marco blows the whistle.
Spot and his friends freeze*

                  Like a statue
Still as a statue
Don't let me catch you
Moving about
Like a statue
Still as a statue
Don't let me catch you
Out!

(*Speaking to the audience*) Now, is anyone moving? Helen's wobbling!
(*Etc.*)

One or two of Spot's friends wobble. The audience shouts out. Marco

*identifies the wobblers. Perhaps Helen has tried a balletic stance that is hard
to sustain. Perhaps Steve has frozen in an acrobatic stance, and topples over*

Good! Thanks everyone!

> (*Singing*) Off you go again now, strut your stuff
> You shake it all about till you're out of puff
> You jig and jog and hip and hop
> But when the whistle
> Blows you have to stop!

All dance

Marco whistles. All freeze

> Like a statue
> Still as a statue
> Don't let me catch you
> Wiggling or giggling or jiggling about
> Like a statue
> Still as a statue
> Don't let me catch you
> Out!

(*Speaking to the audience*) Can you see anyone moving? Yes! Spot's
moving! Mouse too! (*Etc.*) Very good!

Spot Marco, why doesn't— (*he indicates the audience*) everyone play! (*He
indicates his friends*) We could all be the judges!

Marco Why not! (*To the audience*) Your turn now!

All   Come on, ev'rybody, on your feet
                 It's time to play a game that is kind of neat
                 You dance and prance and bounce until
Marco   I blow the whistle
All   And you all stand still!
(*Speaking, ad lib*) Dance! Dance!

*Spot and his friends could go down into the auditorium to encourage the
dancing and do the judging. The House Lights fade up*

The audience dances to the music

Marco whistles. All freeze

> Like a statue
> Still as a statue
> Don't let me catch you
> Moving about
> Like a statue
> Still as a statue
> Don't let me catch you
> Out!

Spot and his friends try to catch members of the audience moving. Eventually...

Marco Very good!

All   Off you go again now, strut your stuff
              You shake it all about till you're out of puff
              You jig and jog and hip and hop
              But when the whistle
              Blows you have to stop!

The audience dances

Marco whistles. All freeze

> Like a statue
> Still as a statue
> Don't let me catch you
> Wiggling or giggling or jiggling about
> Like a statue
> Still as a statue
> Don't let me catch you
> Out!

Again, Spot and his friends try to catch members of the audience moving

Marco Well done! (*Calling Spot and his friends back*) Everybody, one more time! Everybody dance!

Music. All dance. Now Marco blows the whistle at several sudden moments, taking everyone by surprise. Eventually, on the last freeze...

All   Like a statue
              Still as a statue

> Like a statue
> Still as a statue
> Like a statue
> Still as a statue

Marco blows a final whistle

At the end of the game, all cheer and applaud the audience

Marco (*mainly to the audience*) You all did well! You all were best!
Now sit down and have a rest!

The audience begins to settle

Mouse (*suddenly bobbing about*) Eek! Eek! Eek! Eek!
Spot Hallo, Mouse! Did you enjoy that?

Music 40

Mouse dances around then freezes

Very good! Still as a statue!

Mouse unfreezes

Mouse Eek! Eek! Eek! Eek!
Spot What is it?
Helen He's saying maybe we ought to water the seeds again.
All Yes!

All run to the window-box. Spot finds the watering can

Spot Come on, everyone!

Music 41

All & Audience Water the seeds
To make them grow
See if they're growing
Are they?
No!
Sally They won't grow that quickly! I told you!

Music 42

Marco Now, everyone, get ready to play… Hide-and-Seek!

All cheer. Mouse squeaks

And Mouse can play Hide and Squeak!

Music 43

(*Indicating Tom, Steve, Helen, Sally and himself*) We all hide and Spot has
to find us.
Spot Right. (*To the audience*) Will you all help me find them, please?
Audience Yes.
Spot Thank you. But, Marco, when you all hide, what's to stop us seeing?
Marco You close your eyes and count to ten.
Steve And no cheating!
Marco And just to make sure, I'm going to turn out the light!

All react

And, Spot, you can use this to look for us. (*He hands Spot a powerful torch*)
Spot What is it?
Marco A Spot-light! Da daaaaa! Turn it on.

Spot does so

Other lights off! (*He gestures magically*)

Perhaps Sally presses a light switch. The Lights go out. All react

Spot Ooooh! Spooky!

Fun as Spot shines the torch around the auditorium

I can see you! Yoo hoo!
Marco Ready? Eyes closed. Count to ten.
Spot Ready! (*To the audience*) Eyes closed everyone. Count with me.

*During the count, the others hide. They leave part of themselves in vision—
an arm, a foot, Marco's ears?*

*In the original production, Helen hid in the piano, Tom hid in the dressing-
up chest, Sally hid in the cupboard of the dresser, Marco hid in the clock and
Mouse hid under the table. Steve exited, ready to come on later*

One, two, three, four, five, six, seven, eight, nine, ten! Coming, ready or
not!

Music 44

Spot shines the torch and begins to search

*One by one, with Spot helped by the audience, those hiding are discovered.
The audience guess (helped by the colour and appearance of the exposed
limb) who each one is. For example:*

Spot Who's this?
Audience Tom.
Spot Found you, Tom!
Tom Yes!

*Next Sally is found, then Helen, then Mouse (who squeaks to give a clue to
Spot), then Marco*

Spot (*to the audience*) Who's left? Who haven't we found?
Audience Steve!
Spot Steve, yes. Where can he be?

Music 45

From the shadows, Steve, under a tablecloth, emerges, following Spot

*The audience see him and shout out to Spot, who tries to find him, but always
turns the wrong way. He thinks the audience are playing a trick on him*

Eventually Steve throws the tablecloth over Spot and laughs

*Marco turns the Lights on. Spot is thrashing around under the tablecloth. The
others gather round*

Spot (*emerging*) Steve! I knew it was you!
Steve Well done, Spot. You found us all!

Cheers

Spot (*including the audience*) No, *we* did! Thank you, everyone!

Cheers and applause

Sally Now Marco, time for one more game before Spot's birthday cake.

More cheers

Sally exits

Spot What game shall we play, Marco?
Marco Let me think, let me think! Got it! Musical chairs!

Music 46

Cheers. Spot and his friends collect the four blocks, place them c *with 1, 2, 3 and 4 facing front, and sit on them*

You dance around. When the music stops, sit down. If you can't find somewhere to sit, you're out! Off you go!

They play musical chairs as a choreographed musical sequence. Spot, Steve, Helen and Tom dance around. Marco removes a block. The music stops. Fun as they rush to find a seat. Helen is particularly good at the game because she is plumper than the others and can bump them out of the way

In the first round, Tom is out. He is upset, but soon recovers and watches the game continue

Marco removes one of the blocks and Spot, Helen and Steve dance round. When the music stops, Steve is left without a seat. He quickly sits on Helen's lap but Marco intervenes and indicates that Steve is out

Marco removes another block. Only one remains. The music starts again. Marco makes sure Spot and Helen dance around Tom and Steve, each to one side of the stage, rather than "hugging" the block

Nobody, except the audience, sees Sally enter, carrying Spot's birthday cake. She looks for somewhere to put it. She sees the block, puts the cake on it, then exits

The music stops. Spot and Helen dash to the block, sit on the cake and squash it flat

Helen & Spot Aaaaah!

A virtual freeze

Steve What's the matter?
Tom Are you all right?

Sally enters with a cake-slicer

Sally Ready to cut the cake, Spot? (*She stops*) Oh. Where is it?

All look at Helen and Spot who slowly stand, revealing the squashed cake

Oh dear.

Everyone reacts horrified

Helen (*tearfully*) I'm so sorry. I didn't see it. We were playing musical chairs.
Spot That's all right, Helen. We both did it. We didn't see it.
Sally Never mind. (*She comforts Helen and Spot*) It was an accident. Let's
forget about the cake and sing Happy Birthday to Spot anyway.

Music 47

All nod sadly and prepare to sing. Suddenly...

Marco Wait! We can't have a birthday party without a birthday cake!
Sally There's no time to bake another one.
Marco Maybe there is, madam! If we bake it with...

Music 48

...magic!

Enthusiastic response from Spot and his friends

And if everybody helps!
All Yes!
Marco Could I borrow a saucepan, please? A big saucepan?
Sally Certainly.

Sally exits with the squashed cake

Marco (*pointing*) Table!
Spot Table!

Music 49

Steve I'll get it.
Tom I'll help.

They run to fetch the table and bring it c. As they do this...

Marco Cookbook!
Spot Cookbook!

Spot and Helen run to fetch Spot's "cookbook" from the shelf. Steve and Tom bring the table

Steve & Tom Table!
Spot & Helen Cookbook!

Spot and his friends gather round the cookbook

Marco Look up "cakes"!
Spot Cakes!

He starts finding the page, while Marco holds up a magic lunch box

A lunch box.

Marco opens the box and shows it to be empty

Steve There's no lunch in it!
Tom It's empty!
Marco This, my friends, is a...

Music 50

...*magic* lunch box! (*He hands the box to one of Spot's friends to hold*)
Spot (*finding the word in the index*) Cakes! There are lots to choose from!
Steve Banana cake!
Marco Banana cake! Aha! (*He makes a magic gesture*)

Music 51

Abracadabbage!

Marco produces a banana from the magic lunchbox

Marco Banana!

Cheers

From now on, Marco produces each object needed from the lunch box

Music 52

Helen Carrot cake!
Marco Carrot!
Tom Fish cake!
Marco Fish!
Spot Lemon cake!
Marco Lemon!
Helen Orange cake!
Marco Orange!
Tom Sponge cake!
Marco (*producing a bath sponge*) Sponge!
Spot Spot's birthday cake!
Marco Spot's birthday cake! (*He finds nothing in the box*) Ah! We need the recipe.
Spot (*finding it*) Here it is!

Music 53

Spot, followed by his friends, takes the cookbook to Marco

Marco Excellent. Now, follow this recipe. (*He moves from behind the table and walks along, studying the recipe*)

Steve follows and encourages the others to follow too. Marco stops. They bump into him

Aaah! What are you doing?
Steve Following the recipe.

Laughter

Marco No, no. Read the recipe. Read it out, please. (*He passes the book back along the line to Spot, then returns behind the table*)
Spot (*reading*) Take a big saucepan.

Sally enters with a big saucepan

Sally A big saucepan!
Marco Thank you, madam. (*He takes it from her*)
Sally Good luck, everyone.

Sally exits

Marco Next.
Spot Stand on the table.
Marco I beg your pardon?
Spot Stand on the table.
Marco Are you sure?
Spot That's what it says. Stand on the table.
Marco Very well, but it does seem a little odd. (*He puts the saucepan on the ground and stands on the table*)

Music 54

Now what?
Spot Marco, maybe it means stand the saucepan on the table.
Marco Yes, of course! Only joking!

Music 55

He gets down and lifts the saucepan on to the table

Next.
Spot Place the following ingredients into the saucepan.
Steve Two hen's eggs.
Marco I beg your pardon?
Steve Two hen's eggs.

Music 56

Marco makes a magic pass on one of Spot's friends, ideally Tom, putting him in a trance. Then from somewhere about his person, Marco produces a scraggy chicken with long legs

Marco Two hen's legs! (*He makes them dance*)
Steve Not legs. Eggs!
Marco Eggs. Of course. Silly me! Abracadabbage! (*He produces two eggs, one boiled, one fried*) One egg boiled! One egg fried! Two hen's eggs! (*He throws them in*) Next.
Steve Milk!
Marco Milk! (*He produces a bottle of milk from the magic lunch box and throws it in*)
Spot Mixed fruit!
Marco Mixed fruit!

Music 57

He throws in the banana, lemon, and orange he produced before

Banana, lemon, orange! Mixed fruit!

Then, as an afterthought

Carrot! Fish! Why not? (*He throws them in*) Next!
Helen Flour!
Marco Flower!
Helen Flour!
Marco Flower! (*He produces a flower—perhaps it droops*)
Helen Not that sort of flower!

Marco throws it in

Oh well, never mind.
Tom Icing.
Marco Icing? Icing? Ah! I sing! La la la la laaaa! I sing.
Tom No! Icing sugar.
Marco Icing sugar. (*He produces a packet of sugar and tosses it in*)
Spot Take a wooden spoon.

Music 58

Marco Spoon! (*He produces a large wooden spoon*)
Spot And stir…
Marco Stir… (*He starts stirring the air*)
Spot …going round and round.
Marco Going round and round?
Spot Going round and round.
Marco Very well.

Music 59

He revolves on the spot, stirring wildly

Aah! I'm feeling giddy!
Spot Marco, I think it means stir the saucepan.
Marco Of course it does. Just joking!

Music 60

He lowers the spoon into the saucepan and stirs three times, then drops the spoon in

Next.

Spot Heat in an oven for three hours.

Marco Three hours! We can't wait that long. I know! (*To the audience as well as Spot and his friends*) Everybody, please rub your hands together. (*He demonstrates*)

Music 61

Get them really warm.

The others and the audience rub their hands together

Good, that's it! Really hot! Now, hold them up towards the saucepan. Give it lots of heat, enough to cook the cake. (*Perhaps he holds the saucepan and brings it* DS *to receive the heat*) Good, good. I can feel it getting hotter and hotter! Thank you! Now, say after me please. (*He makes magical gestures*)

Music 62

Abracadabbage...

All Abracadabbage...

Marco Carrot and pea...

All Carrot and pea...

Marco Bake us a cake...

All Bake us a cake...

Marco For Spot's birthday tea!

All For Spot's birthday tea!

Marco lifts the lid of the saucepan and brings out a beautiful cake, complete with candles lit

Sally enters in time to see it emerge

All cheer

Sally What a beautiful cake! Well done, Marco!

Marco Everybody helped.

Sally & Spot (*to the audience*) Thank you!

Marco Marco's the name...

All except Marco Magic's your game!

All Da daaaaa!

Sally Come on, everybody…

All gather round

…let's sing a very Happy Birthday to Spot.

Music 63

Song: Happy Birthday, Spot

All, except Spot, lead the audience singing "Happy Birthday" to Spot. Then…

All except Spot & Audience Happy Birthday
                All your friends say
                Happy Birthday, Spot
                Happy Birthday
                You're a good friend
                We love you a lot.

                Happy Birthday
                All your friends say
                Happy Birthday, Spot
                Happy Birthday
                You're a good friend
                The best friend we've got.

Sally & Sam And now the time
                Has come for you
                To make a wish
All except Spot A secret wish…

All turn away except Spot who closes his eyes

Spot   I wish that you
                May always be
                Happy, healthy,
                Lucky as me.

All turn back

All except Spot Happy Birthday
                All your friends say

> Happy Birthday, Spot
> Happy Birthday
> You're a good friend
> We love you a lot.
>
> Happy Birthday
> All your friends say
> Happy Birthday, Spot
> Happy Birthday
> You're a good friend
> The best friend we've got.

Sally holds up the cake

Sally & Sam And now it's time
>   As you well know
>   To take a deep breath...

Spot takes a deep breath

>   And...
All except Spot Blow!

Spot blows the candles. They don't go out

Spot Oh! (*He tries again, without success*) Oh! (*To the audience and his friends*) Please, everybody, help me! Deep breath! One, two, three, *blow*!

All blow. The candles go out. All cheer

Sally I'll cut you all a piece of cake to take home. (*She takes the cake to the table* US)
Tom Is it time to go home?
Sally Yes, it's the end of the party, I'm afraid. It's going home time!

All react

Marco Have you had a good time?
All Yes!
Marco Me too.

Music 64

Steve I like birthdays.

Tom I wish we could have birthdays every day!
Helen They wouldn't be so special then.

During the following song, Marco starts packing his bag

Song: Thank You Song

Sally & Spot Thank you for coming
Steve & Tom & Helen Thank you for having us
Spot   It's been fun
Sally   The time flew by
Spot   Thanks for my presents
                  (*To the audience*) Thanks for my cards
All   Now it's time for us to say goodbye.

Marco (*speaking*) Time for Marco to disappear,
                  Maybe see you all next year!

All (*to Marco*) Thanks for the magic
                  Thank you for all the games
Marco   Glad you liked
                  The things we've done
                  Spot, good to meet you
                  And all your friends
All   Goodbye, Marco.
Marco (*taking in the audience*) Goodbye, ev'ryone!

Marco exits

Tom, Steve and Helen approach. Tom hugs Sally

Tom & Steve & Helen Thanks for the party
                  We've had a brilliant time
Sally & Spot Goodbye, Helen,
                  Tom and Steve.

Sally collects some balloons and hands them out

Sally   Please have a present
                  To play with at home
                  Sorry that it's time for you to leave.

Tom & Steve & Helen We've had a lovely afternoon
                  Bye bye, Spot

See you soon.

(*Speaking to the audience*) Bye!

Steve and Helen leave

Tom lingers

Steve comes back to collect him

Steve Come on, Tom!

Spot (*with a huge yawn*) Thanks for the party
Mum, thanks for ev'rything.
(*Speaking*) Dad, too!
Sally   Who's a tired old
Sleepyhead?
Give me a hand to
Tidy the toys
Then it's time for you to go to bed.

Music continues as they tidy. They reposition the four blocks. For the first time the letters facing front spell "SPOT". Then Sally pulls out Spot's basket. Spot climbs into his basket

Sally (*tucking him in*) Night night, Spot. Sleep tight.
Spot (*yawning*) Night, Mum.

Sally exits

Spot settles down. Suddenly he sits up

(*Calling*) Mum!

Sally enters

Sally Go to sleep, Spot.
Spot Where's my teddy, Mum? Can't sleep without my teddy.
Sally (*finding the teddy in the dressing-up chest*) Here you are. Good night, Spot.
Spot Night, Mum. (*To the audience*) Night!
Audience Night.

Music 65

Spot settles down. Suddenly he sits up

Spot (*calling*) Dad!

Sam enters—or calls from the keyboard

Sam Go to sleep, Spot.
Spot Please can I have a drink of water?
Sam All right. (*As he brings a glass of water*) Did you have a good party?
Spot Great, thanks.
Sam Here you are.

Spot drinks

Spot Thanks, Dad.
Sam Now, go to sleep. Good night, Spot.
Spot Night, Dad. (*To the audience*) Night!
Audience Night!

Music 66

Spot settles down

Suddenly Mouse appears at the window

Mouse Eek! Eek! Eek!
Spot (*sitting up*) Hallo, Mouse. What is it? I'm meant to be asleep!
Mouse Eek! Eek! Eek!
Spot Oh. All right! (*He gets up, finds the watering can and starts to water the seeds. He whispers to the audience*) Say it with me! Not too loud!
All (*whispering*) Water the seeds
To make them grow
See if they're growing
Are they?
No!
Spot Mum's right. They won't grow *that* quickly! (*He goes back to his basket*) Good night, Mouse!
Mouse Eek! Eek! Eek!
Spot (*to the audience*) Night!
Audience Night!

Music 67

Spot settles to sleep

After a pause, music as, from the window box, beautiful sunflowers begin to grow. The Lighting brightens a little

Hopefully the audience shout out the news to Spot, who eventually wakes up and, led by the audience, sees the sunflowers. Maybe more, larger, sunflowers appear from the sides and from above

Spot (*calling*) Mouse!

Mouse appears

  Look!
Mouse (*happily*) Eek! Eek! Eek!
Spot (*calling*) Mum, Dad!

  Sally and Sam enter

Sally & Sam Spot, how many more times? Go to sleep.
Spot Look!

Sally and Sam see the sunflowers

Sally Oh, Spot, they've grown! They're beautiful.
Sam And just in time for your birthday!
Sally Now go to sleep.
Sally & Sam Goodnight, Spot.

  Sally and Sam exit

Spot (*settling down again*) Night, Mum. Night, Dad. Night, Mouse. (*To the audience*) Night!
Audience Night.

Music 68

Pause

Black-out

END OF ACT II

CURTAIN CALL

Music 69

The actors take a bow. Then they sing a final reprise

All except Spot Happy Birthday
                    All your friends say
                    Happy Birthday, Spot
                    Happy Birthday
                    You're a good friend
                    We love you a lot.

                    Happy Birthday
                    All your friends say
                    Happy Birthday, Spot
                    Happy Birthday
                    You're a good friend
                    The best friend we've got.

Spot   Hope you liked my party, party, party
                    Thank you all for joining in the fun
                    Hope you liked my party, party, party
                    Thank you everyone.

All   Hope you liked the party, party, party
                    Thank you all for joining in the fun
                    Hope you liked the party, party, party
                    Thank you everyone.

                    Hope you liked the party, party, party
                    Thank you all for joining in the fun
                    Hope you liked the party, party, party
                    Bye bye everyone.
                    Bye bye everyone.

CURTAIN

FURNITURE AND PROPERTY LIST

Further dressing may be added at the director's discretion

ACT I

On stage: 4 portable screens serving as doors, possibly linked for folding into a
      magic cabinet
Spot's basket
Window-box
Small watering can
Larger watering can
Percussion instruments including cymbals and triangle
Toy instruments including flute
Pink grand piano
Clock
Bookshelf
Dressing-up chest
Cardboard crown for **Spot**
Confetti

Off stage: Children's birthday cards (**SM**)
Ball wrapped as present (**Tom**)
Large box of sunflower seeds wrapped as present (**Helen**)
Drum wrapped as present (**Steve**)
Bag of equipment, long-handled broom (magic prop), magic wand,
      novelty balloons, invitation, wand with star, cardboard crown
      (**Marco**)
Tiny birthday card (**Mouse**)
Large book wrapped as present (**Sally**)
Cut-out rocking horse, large version of child's playcart (**SM**)

Personal: **Marco**: plain-coloured scarf, paper spots, sticky-backed brown spot,
      whistle or harmonica, bunch of flowers (magic prop)

INTERVAL

Set: **Suggested toys**:
                Pedal car
                Hobby horse
                Unicycle
                Space hopper
                Pogo stick
                Skateboard
                Wheelbarrow
                Hula hoop
                Roller blades
                Marco's juggling balls

ACT II

On stage: As before

Set: **Spot**'s teddy bear in dressing-up chest
                Glass of water
                Window box with sunflowers for growing effect

Off stage: **Spot**'s birthday cake (**Sally**)
                Cake-slicer (**Sally**)
                Big saucepan (**Sally**)
                Cake with candles lit (**Marco**)

Personal: **Marco**: powerful torch, magic lunch box, banana, carrot, fish, lemon,
                orange, bath sponge, scraggy chicken with long legs, boiled egg,
                fried egg, bottle of milk, flower, packet of sugar, large wooden
                spoon
                Steve: tablecloth

LIGHTING PLOT

Property fittings required: fake cake candles
1 interior setting. The same throughout

ACT I

To open: House lights on

Cue 1   **Audience** are sitting   (Page 1)
        Cross-fade house lights to stage lighting

Cue 2   **Marco**: "Lights!"   (Page 5)
        Change lighting magically

Cue 3   **All**: "One, two, three!"   (Page 7)
        Flash lights

Cue 4   **All** dance   (Page 10)
        Bring up disco lighting effects

Cue 5   **Marco**: "Lights!"   (Page 24)
        Change lighting dramatically

Cue 6   **Sally**: "Hey presto!"   (Page 26)
        Magical lighting effect

Cue 7   **Sally**: "Wallaballoo!"   (Page 27)
        Magical lighting

Cue 8   **Spot**: "Above the moon is shining bright…"   (Page 27)
        Lighting effect

Cue 9   **Spot** and **Helen** dance   (Page 29)
        Increase lighting on the clock

INTERVAL

To open: House lights on

ACT II

To open: Cross-fade house lights to stage lighting

Cue 10   **Spot and his friends** judge audience dancing   (Page 36)
              Fade up house lights

Cue 11   **Sally** presses light switch   (Page 39)
              Black-out

Cue 12   **Marco** turns lights on   (Page 40)
              Bring up lighting

Cue 13   **Spot** blows cake candles   (Page 49)
              Flutter cake lights

Cue 14   **Spot** tries again   (Page 49)
              Flutter cake lights

Cue 15   **All** blow   (Page 49)
              Cut out candle lights

Cue 16   Sunflowers begin to grow   (Page 53)
              Brighten lighting a little

Cue 17   **Audience**: "Night."   (Page 53)
              After music and pause, black-out

EFFECTS PLOT

ACT I

Cue 1   To open   (Page 1)
           Pre-recorded music

Cue 2   **Marco**: "One, two, three!"   (Page 7)
           Flash effect

Cue 3   **Marco** makes tick-tock noises   (Page 29)
           Turn clock hands through several hours towards midnight

ACT II

Cue 4   **Spot** settles to sleep   (Page 52)
           Make sunflowers grow from window box

MADE AND PRINTED IN GREAT BRITAIN BY
LATIMER TREND & COMPANY LTD PLYMOUTH
MADE IN ENGLAND